the better parts

reflections of love

melonee johnson

ISBN – 13: 978-0-692-05923-4

Cover designed by: Derek Murphy

dedication

We are strong alone, but unbeatable together. This love's no longer fragile; time has toughened it up. Not a fashion or a trend, it's that forever love, that's here to stay.

This book is dedicated to the one who will always have an unguarded space in my heart. Moments matter.

- Melonee Johnson aka RedLoveSong

Contents

acknowledgements...7

the better parts..8

yesterday's soup...9

It's in the verbs..10

back to love...11

give & take..12

what a fire can't consume 13

heart eyes...14

nothing less than butterflies 15

connected..16

listen to your heart..17

unraveled love 18

will you..20

caged bird free 21

back to the basics...22

I want to be...23

heart mail..24

to be. too be. two be. 25

designed for two 26

without effort..27

home away from home.......................................28

speaking of you 29

I love how 30

audience of one..31

radiation 32

completely incomplete 33

like the moon...34

when I will you?..35

I see you...36

You 37

reflection of my heart..38

about the author 39

acknowledgements

First of all, thanks to God for the gift to love and write from the heart.

To the entire Johnson family, we didn't always have a lot, but we were always rich in love, and still are. I am forever grateful to you.

To D'Peate for keeping my pen flowing after all these years, even in my season of drought. You are my pen's soulmate.

To every past love, good or bad, I wouldn't be the writer/lover that I am without you.

To everyone who purchases this book, thanks for supporting the best part of me: love.

To my future love/muse, I am patiently waiting for you to come inspire my best work ever.

the better parts

though many have tales of sorrow
pain, hurt and misery
I choose to record my experience
of the better parts of love
& all of its glory
when butterflies inhabited the tummy
& even the corniest jokes were funny
when motives and intentions were always so pure
& your faith in that someone was equally sure
when you believed that love had the potential to last
& your new love wasn't a victim of your past
when giving was way more honorable than receiving
& telling the truth was more common than deceiving
those tales of hurt, misery and pain
are those not of true love
so on her please don't place blame

yesterday's soup

like yesterday's soup
love should be rich and layered
with blended goodness
the particulars of them
mixed with the essence of you
to create something worth savoring
their experience, patience & wit
combined with your energy, honesty & kindness
seasoned with a handful of trust
a cup of clever conversation
some spicy stimulation & a lot of spiritual inspiration
mutual praise and a raw connection
stirred with pure intuition
simmered slowly with the heat of passion
over time will create a love so flavorful & satisfying
that you'll desire nothing else

It's in the verbs

for me it's not the words
It's in the actions shown
I know you say you mean it
but until I feel it, it's not truly known

like when you call to say you care
through your touch, I know you're there
love for me is in the little things
so much pleasure your kisses bring

homemade soup when I'm not feeling good
comforting words when I'm misunderstood
support for the things that bring me bliss
unselfish love is the sum of this

so it's not in the number of syllables spoken
It's in the amount of promises unbroken
now I do admit I must hear the words
but love without action is for the birds

back to love

I'm finally getting back to love
to the place my heart knows best
where feelings of peace reside
& joy overwhelming abides

you know the place
where the lyrics in songs
seem to speak directly to your heart
& not just a small part

like they were written
from the very pages of your diary
the lines you swore never to share
but it feels like the artist was standing right there

looking over your shoulder
peeking into the chambers of your soul
revealing to the world your inner most secrets
your future dreams of "to have and to hold"

I'm finally getting back to love
to the place my heart knows best
where moments matter more than words
& I'm feeling liberated like the birds

give & take

my weakness
your strength
your faults
my compliments
you talk
I listen
my opinion
our decision
you give
I take
I give
you appreciate
my eyes
for you
your heart
stays true
my song
you sing
your bell
I ring
you fight
I fight
we'll be alright

what a fire can't consume

what you have
where you live
matters not
for it can easily be taken away

what you say
what you do
matter most
and is what gets me through my day

give me not
what can be destroyed
or consumed in a fire

give me what remains
when the ashes settle
your heart is what I desire

heart eyes

I see with my heart
what's invisible to the eye
and oblivious to the mind
you should try it sometime
let your heart dictate
where your love should grow
the place your mind
doesn't relate
where you let your feelings show
then tell me what you see
when you look at me

nothing less than butterflies

here I am in love
dreams of forever
are stranded in my mind
maybe a world of make believe in your eyes
but I am not who you want me to be
I bestow love
and love lies at my feet
come fly away with me
I'll give you a reason to believe
inject my love into your veins
make you scribe unspoken dreams
of nothing less than butterflies
midnight kisses & sweet lullabies
dreams are memories we have forgotten
but a scent can surely remind you of bliss
the warmth of an embrace
the spark in a kiss
beneath your silent whispers and hidden cries
you truly believe that love never dies
you just don't understand why
and neither do I
but I do know that
love has always proven me right
and I'll settle for nothing less than butterflies

connected

over 1250 miles away by car
six hours with two stops by plane
about fifty dollars over
a week's worth of pay
the time and cost is minimal
when you factor in the connection
now that's priceless

you're worth every minute
I'd spend alone in the car driving
every aching pain in my body
while in that cramped seat on the plane
every cent I earned to spend
while working those boring hours
If it means that I'd get a chance
just for a moment
to be in your presence

listen to your heart

I am patiently waiting for you
the one I need to love
the one who can receive my love
it is no mistake
I accept no defeat
when it comes to matters of the heart
I will not retreat
the mind is deceiving
for what is best
I know you feel
what I'm trying to express
I hope you see the visible path
straight to the arms of your desire
I was made to release you from your bondage
created to relieve you of your pain
inject my love into your veins
summon you back to life
renew your spirit
revive your soul
restore your energy
simply make you whole
my heart beats only for you
as I patiently wait for you to
listen not to what I speak
but to your own heartbeat
as the rhythm moves
in time with mine
echoing loud and clear
a harmony so sublime

unraveled love

not patient by nature
but when it comes to love
I have an inherited endurance

it seems I will wait for the right thing
instead of settle for the wrong thing
As long as it may take

you see

love to me is more than a feeling of butterflies
sugar laced conversations
illusions of perfect days and nights
"don't wake me, I'm dreaming" replies

love is letting me unravel you
without fear of rejection of your unmasked self
chasing dreams together
without a final destination in sight
giving to each other
more than any love song could ever convey
savoring moments
the little things
that take my breath away

do you feel my heartstrings?
can you hear the song my heart sings?
listen with your heart's ears
and put that song on repeat

will you

will you let go of the past
& let your present love you right
will you openly receive the happiness you speak of
if only for one night?

will you entrust your heart to another
who only knows how to give
will you let down your guard
in a place designed for you to live

will you believe the words of the one
who promises to bring no pain
will you allow yourself to be
completely saturated in love's rain

will you let fear and control take a back seat
to the joy that makes you smile
will you let your heart lead your mind
if only for a while

caged bird free

let my tree offer the shade that your heart truly needs
let my hands stitch up the places, the spaces where it bleeds

let my water(fall) and refresh the dryness that you feel
let my love suffocate the bitterness so that your heart can heal

let my morning bring the sun and warm your chilly days
let my voice cry out your name to God every time I pray

let my river flow to you and calm your raging sea
let my love simply set your caged bird free

back to the basics

let's go back to the start
when this thing was effortless
where it flowed like honey from a comb
let's go back to that place
that we never wanted to leave
late nights and early mornings

your love has always been in season
available when I've needed it most
has helped to keep my faith in it
when I wanted to lose hope
your love has always been soothing
like a blanket on a cold night

sweet & satisfying
never one to give up
forever grateful I am
for the gift of your love
and the gift to share my love with you
you'll never know the extent
that you truly mean to me

I want to be

simply
you're my weakness
I'm powerless in your presence
like the golden rays of the sun
I'm drawn to your warmth
absorbing the energy you supply
I yearn to be near you
under your spell I am
it's no secret obsession
though unspoken is a desire known
and equally shared
the truth is in all the words we never say
but felt in every inviting sunrise
and every magnetic sunset
somewhere along the way
you've given me a renewed hope
in the joy that love brings
you've taught me to savor the moments
bask in the essence of it
and to get lost in the passion of the heart
love deserves to be alive
and she is alive in me
so here's my moment of truth
I want to be in love
but I only want to be in it with you

heart mail

days go by & I find myself hooked
on the memory of your voice
I know you're busy with work
but I can't help but wonder
if I cross your mind as many times
as you do mine

impatient am I
as I wait for the mail to arrive
in breathless anticipation
ready to open your letter
written from your soul
to mine

I take my time reading
in order to savor the meaning
behind your every word
I feel your heart
In every single line

to be. too be. two be.

to be with the one you adore
most in the world
at the moments that matter most
is what the heart desires
but is not always
what the heart gets

too be doing the one thing
that brings you the most joy
creating moments that matter
is what the soul needs
but is not always
what the soul gets

two be as one
bringing each other closer
to what the heart desires
& what the soul needs
are moments that we share
& why I'll always love you

designed for two

I love how you pursue me
in sync with the rhythm of my heartbeat
adding harmony to this sweet melody
I don't stop the path I'm on
but I slow down just enough
to let you catch up
and you never miss a beat

we're stupid together
but way too passionate to care
what anyone else thinks
they wouldn't understand us anyway
cause the love language we share
was designed just for two
me and you
tnt

without effort

sexy without effort
at any time of day
that's just your way
I just admire how you stay
captivating
morning, noon and night
I can call at 2am
and your voice tends to excite
sounds just right
makes me feel light
headed
your words stay embedded
into my seams
it seems
I mean
you're stitched into
the fabric of my being
and I be meaning
not to get addicted
but I am
and could have predicted it
from the moment
I first encountered you
and the sexy things you do
just by being you

home away from home

you are my private sanctuary
my oasis after a hard day
my personal escape
when I need to get away
your eyes so welcoming and serene
and voice with its calming effect
you nurture this space in my heart for you
you keep me in peaceful place
I'm content in your embrace
you inspire an intimate space
when I'm in your presence
so warm and inviting
your words send tranquil energy through me
creating a lasting radiant mood
your love is soothing and refreshing
you are my safe haven
my home away from home

speaking of you

thoughts are drawn
to the breaking of dawn
in all of its splendor
its presence
reminds me of your heart's warmth
& the power you possess
to make me desire nothing more
than to be perfectly still
& bask in your gracious glow
your brilliance few will ever know
you are the reflection of my heart
& mirror to my naked soul
beautiful pain shared
in the midst of love's rain
showers you bring
how you make my heart sing
when I speak of you
& only of you

I love how

I love how you let love
be love
and let love
love you

I love how deep
your emotions run
but how very simply
you speak the truth

I love how you demand
my heart
to open and receive
I love that you give me a reason
to once again believe

I love how your poetry teases
& gives your readers just a taste
I love that at the core of me
you have garnered an unguarded space

I love how you share your soul
through your pen
for the whole world to see
but behind closed doors
in your most vulnerable state
you save the very best for me

audience of one

you have me singing new notes
that have yet to be written
in sync with my constant and pure melody
you
without effort
provide the much needed harmony
no one else will get this song
they won't understand the lyrics
they can't even feel the beat
'cause it's not for them
it's a song written only for the heart of you

MELONEE JOHNSON

radiation

I can sit in the darkness
and still see the shine in your eyes
your light shines from within
and radiates through your smile
the earth doesn't need the sun
when you, my love, are around
the energy of your soul
I've been blessed to have found

completely incomplete

what's a king
without a queen
or a queen
without her king
a puzzle without a piece
hannibal without clarice
there's something missing
completely incomplete
your truth be beautiful
truth be refreshing
be what my heart needed
to feel today
be what my ears needed
to hear you say
the very core of you
is so appealing
your presence lingers
it remains, it's secure
it soothes, it uplifts
it's my remedy, elixir
the ultimate cure

like the moon

he said he loves
my cotton soft skin
and midnight kisses
when he's away
he admits he misses
the raspy in my voice
and of course
he has no choice
but to think of my smile
that lingers for a while
longer than he'll fully disclose
but he already knows I know
the extent of his admiration
though I need no declaration
he tells me anyway
cause it brightens my day
to know the truth
he's my Boaz & I'm his Ruth
and since tomorrow's not promised
we embrace our time
moments to be exact
like the moon just knows to glow
he & I
just let our love flow

when I will you?

when I have forgotten
the words to the song in my heart,
will you sing them back to me?

when I feel that I have messed up
and don't deserve to be forgiven,
will you give me a second chance?

when memories of long ago creep back in
and take me to a dark place,
will you pray me through until I see the light?

when I feel insecure
and try to compare myself to others,
will you remind me that I'm a masterpiece, one-of-a-kind?

when I feel backed into a corner
by people who don't understand me,
will you stand up for me and be my voice?

when its only you and I left
looking old, gray and into each other's eyes
will you still love me as much as you do today?

I see you

I see you
in your seasoned years
somewhere in the country
with a cool breeze
sitting on the porch
of a well built house
with a big ol' yard
sipping on some cold sweet tea
sucking on some sunflower seeds
with the warmest smile on your face
enjoying your grandkids
as they run around and play

I see you
happy & quite content
with not a care in the world
enjoying the moments as they unfold
holding hands with your favorite girl
still in love after all these years
there's no place she'd rather be
& that she looks a lot like me
just a well aged queen
laughing and carrying on
at complete and utter peace
I see you and baby I see me

You

you
feed me

you
fill me up

you
hold me

you
never let me go

you
muse me

you
write me love

you
love me

you
are forever loved

reflection of my heart

you are the reflection of my heart
the passion that flows so naturally
I am full to the brim
with pure gratefulness
for the privilege to inhabit the same time and space
with the likes of you
even the shadowed pieces of you
speaks to the lover in me
you are the reflection of my heart
my blue sky on a misty day
sunshine breaking through the clouds
after a heavy rain
you are a comforting hug after experiencing pain
you make my dimples deeper
every time I see your face
you are the definition of amazing
simply
the reflection of my heart

about the author

Melonee Johnson is simply a lover of words. English was always one of her favorite subjects in school, so it just felt natural to write. Reading of course sparked her desire to write and so the two of them went hand in hand. The more she read, the more she wrote. At first they were merely random thoughts, but she began to piece them together to create her own style of poetry. No rhyme, no reason. In 2008, she became affiliated with a poetry site, and it opened her eyes to so many different styles and genres. It helped her pen to flourish. Being inspired by the work of others, helped her to write raw and unfiltered about love and other topics, but love seemed to be her favorite topic. Writing under the pseudonym, RedLoveSong, she was able to write from a pure place and share with her poetry family without judgement, but with great praise and encouragement. After years of doubt, she finally has the courage to share it with the world. This is her first published book and she has plans to share more of her work in the near future. Born and raised in Texas, Melonee is part of a large, close-knit family from South Texas that has been a major influence on her views about love and life. She hopes to influence the world, to love more deeply and genuinely, one moment at a time.

www.ingramcontent.com/pod-product-compliance
Lightning Source LLC
Chambersburg PA
CBHW031531040426
42445CB00009B/487